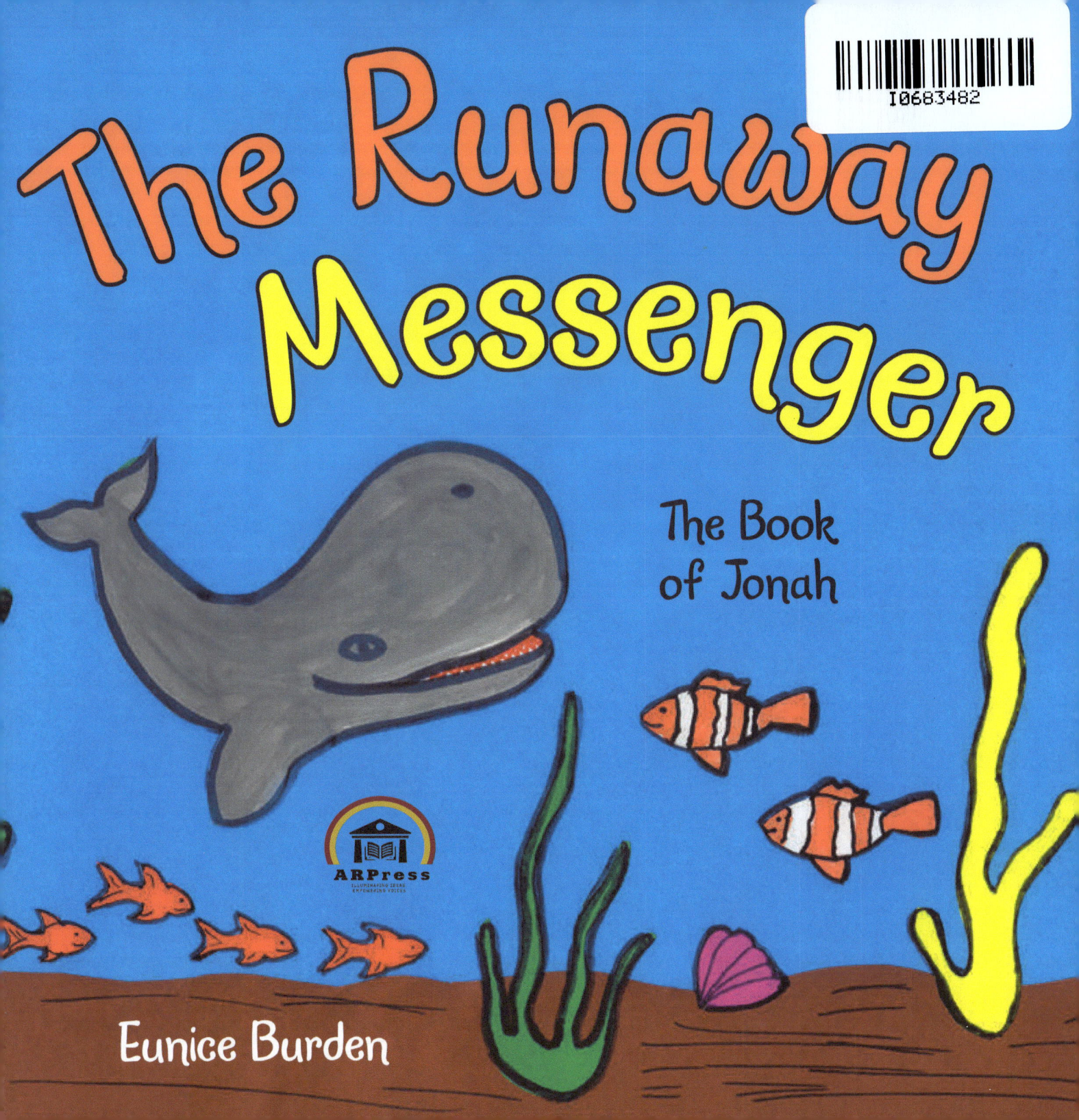

The Runaway Messenger

The Book
of Jonah

Eunice Burden

ARPress
45 Dan Road Suite 5
Canton MA 02021

Hotline: 1(800) 220-7660
Fax: 1(855) 752-6001

Ordering Information:
Quantity sales. Special discounts are available on quantity purchases by corporations, associations, and others. For details, contact the publisher at the address above.

Printed in the United States of America.

ISBN-13:   Softcover   979-8-89389-586-5
                 eBook   979-8-89389-587-2

Library of Congress Control Number: 2024920922

The Runaway Messenger

> The book of Jonah

EUNICE BURDEN

A summary of the book of Jonah in rhyme, for children of ages 6yrs + to listen to as someone reads for them, and then to read for themselves.

I know a tale

About a great big whale,

It started with a man, Jonah was his name

He ended up in trouble, with just himself to blame

One day, Jonah was out walking, as he often used to do

And heard God speaking to him saying "I have a job for you".

Jonah was so glad that God would choose

Him to take a message to the Jews,

But God said "No. The message for today,

Is for a people a long way away."

"Oh, who could that be Lord?" Jonah said

God replied, "not Jews, but Ninevites instead."

'O no, thought' Jonah, 'that's not good.'

Maybe he'd misunderstood.

The message was so clear and plain

"Turn from your sin—serve God again"

But Jonah thought, 'God shouldn't show them love,

He should punish them all from heaven above.'

Jonah thought 'those nasty people should not get this news'

So he turned away and planned a cruise.

Instead of heading for Ninevah city

He went to Joppa, which was a pity.

For Jonah would soon come to know

That wherever God sends you, you must go.

A ship was bound for Tarshish, its cargo safely stored

So Jonah asked the price, paid his fare, and jumped aboard.

Once on the ship he climbed down nice and deep

And found a comfy place to sleep

Out to sea and far away

It seemed a perfect sailing day

When out of nowhere came a squall

Frightening the crew members, one and all.

To keep the ship as light as could be

They threw the cargo into the sea

And there they saw in the cargo pile

Jonah! He'd slept all the while.

"Get up my man" the captain said

"We need your help, it's not time for bed!"

Ask your God, "This storm, who is to blame?

Tell your God to give the man's name".

But Jonah knew who was to blame
And told them all with guilt and shame.
"The storm has come because of me
The cure is, throw me into the sea."

So for his sin, Jonah had to pay
The sailors could find no other way.
He sunk in the sea cold, dark and dim
But God sent a big fish to rescue him

While he was there with no food or drink

Jonah had a lot of time to think

He prayed "O Lord, what a stupid thing to do

To think I could run away from you."

Three days inside the fish he passed

Then Jonah on a beach was cast

God came to Jonah on that day

Gave him one more chance to obey.

"The people of Ninevah must repent!"

So with this message Jonah's sent.

He went at once and preached to all.

Everyone repented, both great and small

"Please God, forgive our foolish ways

And we will offer you our praise"

God heard their prayer and smiled from above

He forgave their sins, because of his love

23

Jonah, on the other hand

Was cross that God should save their land,

Because God forgave it made him sad,

These people really are so bad.

He did not want God to forgive,

They should be punished and no longer live.

Jonah sat and watched outside the city

Where he'd be able to look and see.

Would God destroy this nasty place

Or show his love and grant them grace?

The hot sun shone on the camp he'd made

So God sent a gourd to give him shade

But after that, the very next day

God sent a worm, to eat it away.

Jonah grumbled at God– "Lord, that's not fair

My shade has gone, Lord, don't you care?"

But God spoke to Jonah out of love

And asked him a question from above.

"You want me to help because you suffer,

But do not care about another,

There are thousands of people in Ninevah's city

Couldn't you even show some pity?"

"For I made all those people there

And so I love them and I care

It matters to me when one of them dies

You need to see them through my eyes."

Across the world are billions of people

God made them and he loves them all

He calls them to turn from their wicked ways

And turn to him to sing his praise.

If you know the Saviour, if you love his name

He asks you to join his people, his good news proclaim

It is not always easy, some won't understand

But God says he'll be with you and guide you by his hand.

www.ingramcontent.com/pod-product-compliance
Lightning Source LLC
Chambersburg PA
CBHW041606120626
46551CB00002B/334